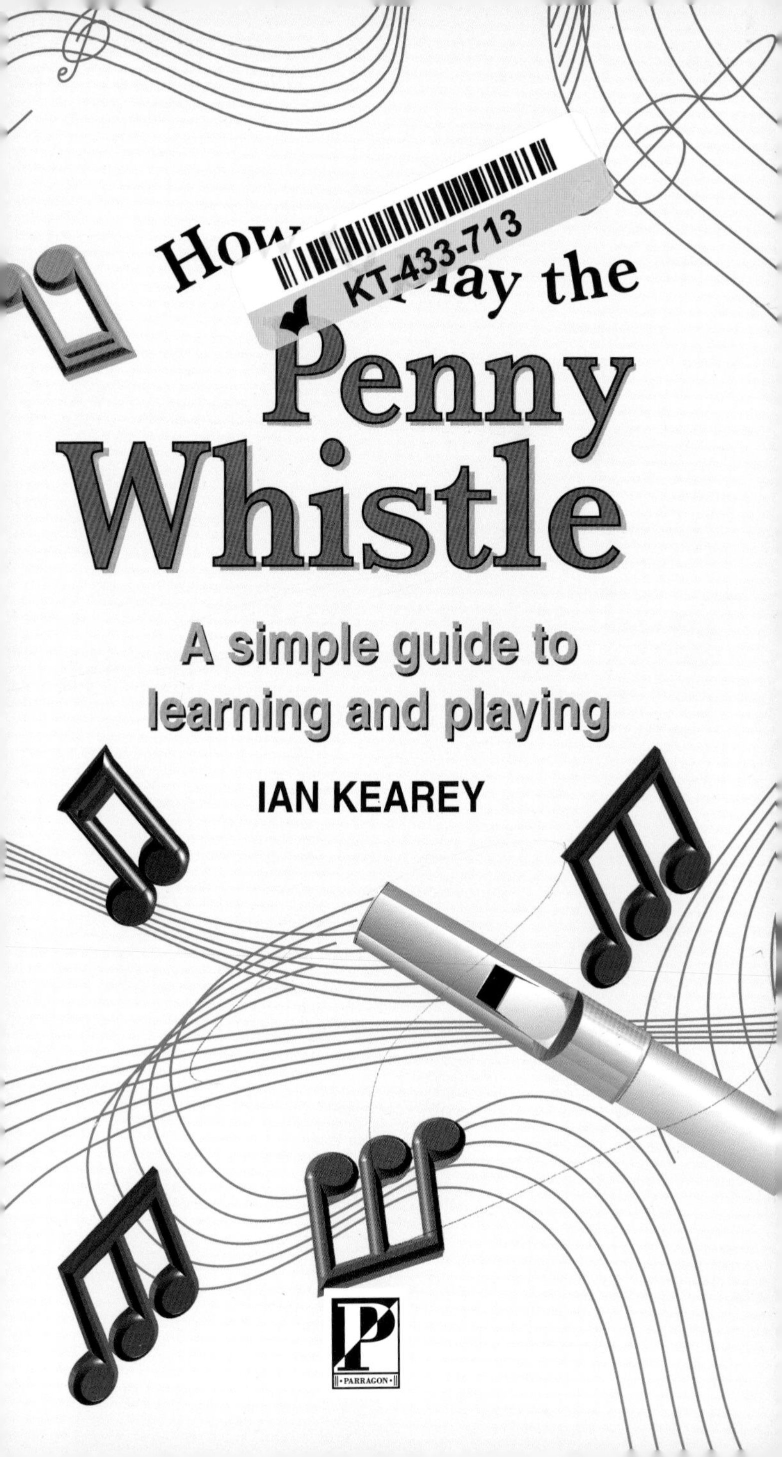

How
lay the
Penny
Whistle
A simple guide to
learning and playing
IAN KEAREY
PARRAGON

First published in Great Britain by

Parragon

13 Whiteladies Road

Clifton

Bristol BS8 1PB

ISBN: 0-75252-508-5

Printed in China

Produced by Haldane Mason, London

Acknowledgements

Art Director: Ron Samuels

Editor: Charles Dixon-Spain

Designer: Zoë Mellors

Illustrator: Stephen Dew

Notation: Lancaster Music Notation

Picture acknowledgements:

Redferns: 15; Mick Hutson 8, 44; S. Moore 18, 59; O. Noel 14; Barbara Steinwehe 16. *Werner Forman Archive:* 10, 11 (both).

Contents

Introduction

Penny whistle, tin whistle, Irish whistle, flageolet – all names for a simple wind instrument that conjures up a wealth of musical images. From the bounce and rhythm of reels and jigs at an Irish ceilidh *or country dance, to the plaintive slow airs and melodies of a solo player, the sound of the penny whistle is heard as much today as it ever was in the past; and the modern street performer or busker with his or her penny whistle is in a direct line from the street hawkers and travelling pedlars who used to play tunes to attract prospective purchasers of their inexpensive instruments.*

Because it is the easiest of the recorder family to learn, for many years the penny whistle was regarded by the musical establishment as not worthy of the attention of serious or accomplished musicians; it was suitable as a present for children or as a Christmas stocking filler that might lead to an interest in a 'proper' instrument, but not much more in its own right. The fact that many hundreds of thousands have been bought, quickly learned and enthusiastically played gives the lie to such musical snobbery. Today, the revival of interest in traditional musics of all countries and cultures has brought the penny whistle and its various cousins back to prominence, and virtuoso players have earned the respect of musicians and critics of all disciplines.

By learning to play the penny whistle, you will join the thousands of others who value the instrument for its clarity of tone and beauty of expression. Don't forget, though, that you have to work at it – competence doesn't arrive immediately, and that's where this book comes in. Stick with it, and the satisfaction of being able to play what you want, when and where you want, will quickly repay the study and practice you put in. Above all, enjoy playing your penny whistle and going through the learning process – once you get started, it's hard to put the penny whistle down!

How to use this book

The techniques of playing and tunes featured in the following pages are based around a standard six-hole penny whistle tuned to the key of D i.e. the penny whistle will play notes which are related to one another in a scale, known as 'the key of D'. However, penny whistles can be easily adapted to penny whistles tuned to other keys (penny whistles are manufactured in the keys of C, D, Eb, F, G and Bb). The aim of the book is to provide the complete beginner, with no musical training or knowledge, with a simple guide to playing the melodies of well-known songs and tunes; as well as introducing more advanced and complex techniques and a selection of traditional tunes that are particularly suited to the penny whistle.

When you first start playing the penny whistle, you may be surprised at how quickly you can play simple tunes without needing to read them from standard musical notation; in addition, many famous penny whistle players have never learned to read music, and 'play by ear'. However, not everyone has the facility to pick up a tune from hearing it, and a basic knowledge of reading music is invaluable in the long run, so persevere with the information given in Chapter 2 and it will pay dividends in expanding your repertoire.

Although the aim of this book is to enable you to read tunes from any written source, the tunes featured here also include notation that has been developed for the beginner on the penny whistle. The penny whistle is shown as seen from the front:

Penny whistle with all holes uncovered

When all six holes are covered by the fingers, the penny whistle is shown thus, and the number 6 is shown either on its own or with standard notation:

Penny whistle with all holes covered

Using this notation, the notes of the bottom octave are:

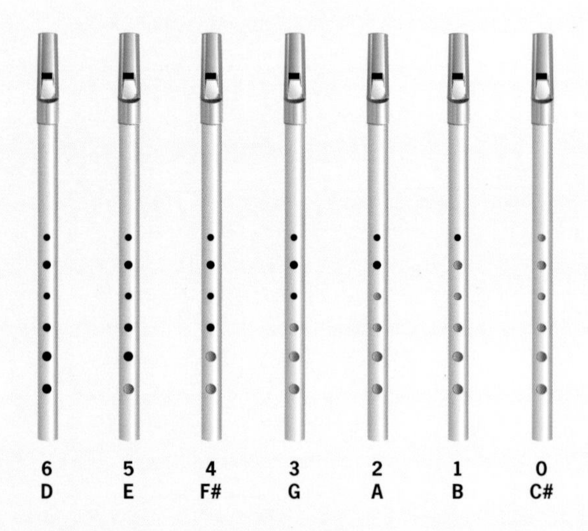

For the top octave, which is produced by overblowing (*see* Chapter 2), the numbers are shown within circles:

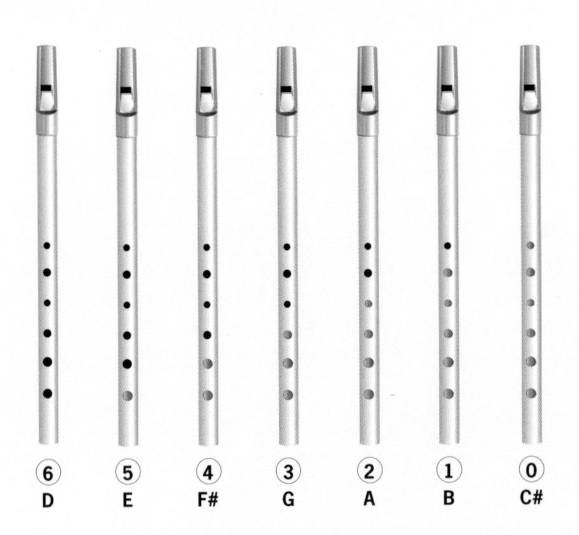

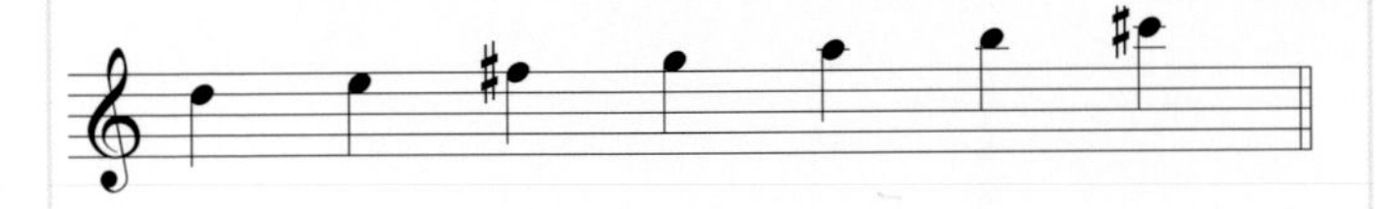

Further instructions and variations are given in the relevant sections.

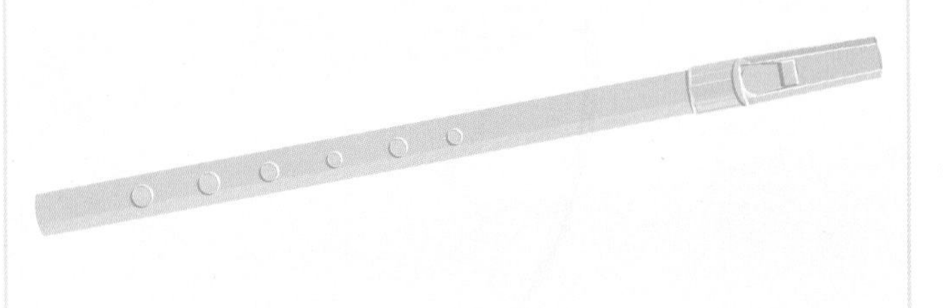

Chapter **1**

About the penny whistle

'pen•ny•whistle n 1: a small fipple flute 2: a toy whistle'

Merriam-Webster's Collegiate Dictionary, 10th ed., 1995

The Pogues combine the penny whistle with a full rock rhythm section.

A brief history

The penny whistle is the modern version of one of the oldest types of instruments known to mankind: simple end-blown flutes made from wood, clay, bone (both animal and human), reeds, cane and metal have been discovered at archaeological sites all over the world. These range from having two or three holes to six or eight, and from being crudely fashioned to elaborately ornamented. Some are assumed to have been used in religious ceremonies or the imitatation of bird calls, but the majority are thought to have had a purely social use.

In the Middle Ages and after, a primitive version of the penny whistle, the pipe or galoubet, was played throughout Europe, usually accompanied by a small side drum, the tabor or tambourine. This pipe had three finger holes and was played with the right hand, while the tabor was beaten with the other; the combination was used for country and morris dancing. Recorders were popular in Western high-art music from about the sixteenth century to the late eighteenth, at which time they were largely supplanted by side-blown flutes. Their close cousin, the flageolet, was in vogue well into the nineteenth century, and the penny whistle as we know it was first produced in the early nineteenth century, when mass-manufacturing methods could be used to

This chinese figure holding a flute dates from before the tenth century.

The Maoris of New Zealand used open-tube flutes or *ngums*.

produce large numbers of accurately pressed, rolled and hole-punched instruments.

In an attempt to bring a touch of class to a simple and very cheap instrument, these early penny whistles were often marketed and sold as 'flageolets' – some are still called by that name today – but the name 'penny whistle' quickly became the norm. They were sold by travelling pedlars and as children's toys, and were taken up by street musicians and thousands of enthusiastic amateurs. The modern penny whistle was perfected in the early years of the twentieth century, when a seamless tube was first used, and the standard plastic mouthpiece was added. In the 1920s and 1930s, penny whistles enjoyed a vogue in northern Europe, particularly among schoolchildren, and many classes were started. The folk music revival of the 1950s and 1960s brought the penny whistle to new generations of players, and its popularity today is as great as it has ever been.

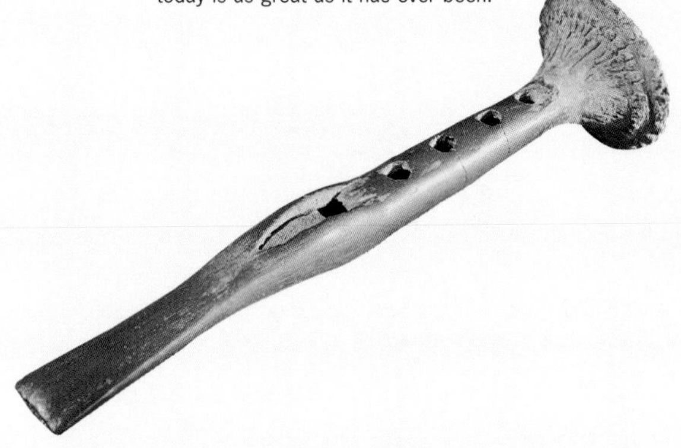

Small flutes and flageolets have been found thoughout the sites of the Aztec empire.

How it works

Despite its inexpensiveness and humble origins, the modern penny whistle is a highly engineered and accurately machined instrument. The separate mouthpiece, made of wood or moulded plastic, is designed to fit the player's mouth comfortably. Older penny whistles were made in one piece, but the metal mouth opening could be sharp or badly made; for this reason, these are not recommended. The tube is manufactured from brass, and is sometimes nickel-plated – James Galway's favourite penny whistles are gold-plated! – with the finger holes punched out of the seamless metal. The tube is lacquered and finished to give a plain, shiny appearance; some players like to add their own patterns and decorations.

When the end of the mouthpiece is blown, the hole at the top directs the air down the tube. This vibrates as a column of air inside the tube and the note emerges through the top mouthpiece hole. The length of the tube determines the key of the penny whistle, and when the finger holes are covered, they lengthen and shorten the amount of air allowed to travel freely, thus raising and lowering the notes.

Although the penny whistle is rightly thought of as one of the most portable of all instruments, to be carried anywhere and played at a moment's notice, it is still worth taking care of it, as rough or careless handling can damage it irreparably. If the brass tube becomes bent or is dented, the penny whistle will not play all its notes accurately, if at all, so treat it with respect and handle it gently – even if a spoon can't be found, don't use a penny whistle to stir your coffee! In the same way, a mouthpiece that is chewed, bashed or dropped will eventually cease to function. The best way to carry one or more penny whistles about is to purchase or make a single or multiple case from sturdy cloth or canvas, making sure that each whistle has its own snug-fitting compartment, to avoid accidental knocks and dents.

As with any instrument, there are many tricks of the trade that players swear by – and as with all instruments, some of these are not really based on commonsense practice. The habit of leaving either the tube or mouthpiece in a glass of beer or rum and blackcurrant may give the penny whistle a more attractive taste, but it will ultimately clog up the instrument, leading to a loss of both tone and accuracy in the notes. Some experienced players like to twist the mouthpiece around on the brass tube to free it a little, and set the exact pitch of the notes by setting it higher or lower on the tube; however, modern penny whistles are manufactured with great precision, and it is highly unlikely that you will buy a faulty one, so it is best to concentrate your efforts on learning and playing.

When you first start playing, and until you have mastered the technique of tonguing, you may find that quite a bit of saliva travels into the mouthpiece. If this is the case, hold the end of the tube and gently shake out the saliva or tap the mouthpiece gently but firmly on your free hand or leg. Clean the brass tube by rubbing gently with a soft, lint-free cloth.

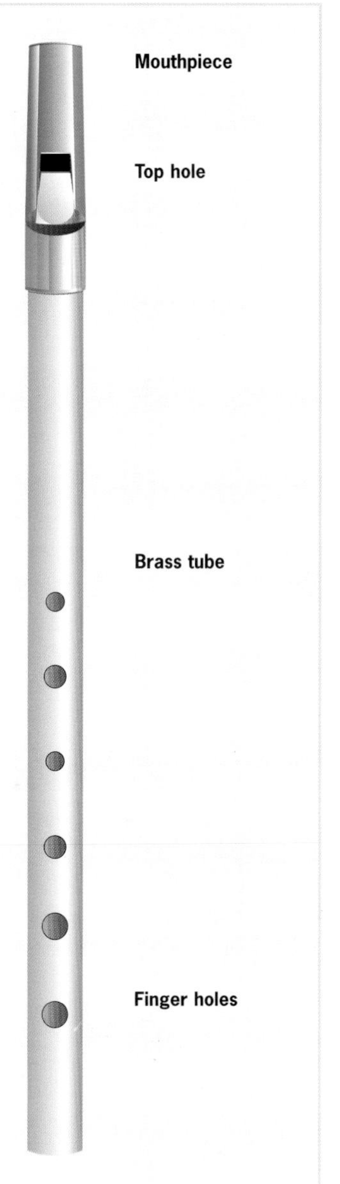

The penny whistle family

The penny whistle is a member of the family of musical instruments known as aerophones, where sound is produced by the vibration of a column of air. Aerophones include brass instruments such as the saxophone, trumpet and tuba, but the penny whistle belongs to another sub-group, the woodwind family. Here, some instruments, for example the oboe, bassoon and clarinet, use separate reeds inserted into the body of the instrument to produce the column of air. However, the simplest method of vibrating a column of air is for a player to blow directly into, or across, a mouthpiece that is an integral part of the instrument; flutes and fifes are side-blown, but the penny whistle is end-blown.

The most commonly seen end-blown instruments in the Western world, apart from the penny whistle itself, are the flageolet and the various recorders – descant, treble, alto, tenor and even bass – some of which use metal sprung keys and mouthpieces to produce the full range of notes. In addition to these, there are a number of variants found in Europe, including the dvojnice from the Balkan region, which has twin tubes made out of wood, both of which have finger holes, and the little ocarina, first made in

Tenor and bass recorders were developed in medieval times.

Italy in the nineteenth century. This is made from fired clay, and its popularity has spread to other continents. As with the examples below, each of these has a unique sound, according to the materials used and the design.

Other members of the end-blown family include the nay, used throughout the Middle East and North Africa, and the twin-tubed zummara, also found in North Africa. The pungi of Northern India, the traditional snake-charmer's pipe, also has two tubes, one of which is tuned to a single note and played as a drone against the melody of the other. The Andean region of South America has the kena or qena, a larger, ornately decorated version of the penny whistle made from hollow cane, and its bass counterpart, the kenacha or qenacha; and the Japanese shakuhachi is the best-known member of the family in South-East Asia.

Peruvian and Bolivian *kenas* are admired throughout the world for their haunting sound.

Chapter **2**

The basics of playing

'Give the piper a penny to play, and twopence to leave off.'

Thomas Fuller, Gnomologia, 1732

James Galway is as proficient on the penny whistle as he is on the flute.

Holding and blowing

Many people imagine that getting a sound out of a penny whistle is simply a matter of holding it, putting their fingers roughly over some of the holes and blowing as hard as possible. However, this is far from the truth – as trying it this way proves instantly! As with any musical instrument, there are right ways and wrong ways – let's ignore the latter and concentrate on getting it right.

Start by sitting up straight. Place the end of the mouthpiece between your lips, making sure that you don't cover the hole at the top of the mouthpiece. With the brass tube resting on your left thumb, cover holes 1, 2 and 3 with the soft pads of the index, middle and ring fingers of your left hand (*see* page 9). Cover holes 4, 5 and 6 with the index, middle and ring fingers of your right hand, using your right thumb to gently grip the tube. Keep your fingers almost straight, and hold the penny whistle angled slightly down from the horizontal position.

Hold the penny whistle at an angle that is comfortable for you.

To produce a steady note, take a normal breath and breathe evenly down the mouthpiece. If you get a shrill note mixed in with this, bring your hands down a little and try again until you achieve the right note. If you blow too hard, the result will be a high, shrieking sound; too soft, and the note will waver.

When you can produce a pleasant, even sound, take your right ring finger off the hole, thus covering five holes, and blow again. Then take the right middle finger off its hole and play that note; continue taking your fingers off the holes until they are all off, resting the tube on your thumbs. Now play the following exercise, playing as fast or slow as you like:

6 6 5 5 4 4 5 5 4 4 3 3

4 4 3 3 2 2 1 1 0 0 1 1

2 2 3 3 2 2 4 4 3 3 5 5

4 4 5 5 6 6 4 4 2 2 6 6

To provide more definition to the notes, begin each one by tonguing it: to tongue a note or series of notes, start by raising your tongue in your mouth and making the sound 'too' as you blow. Play the exercise again, first tonguing each note, then every second note, every third one, and then every fourth one.

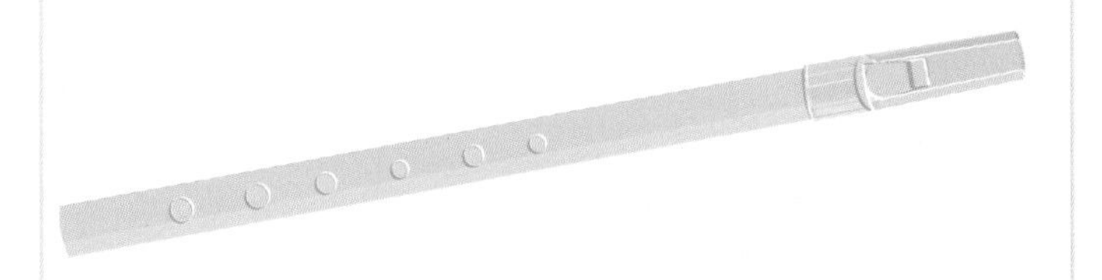

Playing the notes

When you are able to produce steady notes, you are ready to play simple tunes. These should be familiar to you, so you should know which notes are shorter or longer. Practice them, tonguing where you feel it necessary – tonguing every single note can sound monotonous, so create variety by using one breath for more than one note.

Frère Jacques

6 5 4 6 6 5 4 6

4 3 2 4 3 2

2 1 2 3 4 6

2 1 2 3 4 6

6 5 6 6 5 6

When the Saints go Marching In

6 4 3 2 6 4 3 2

6 4 3 2 4 6 4 5

4 4 5 6 6 4 2 2 3

4 3 2 4 6 5 6

London Bridge

2 1 2 3 4 3 2

5 4 3 4 3 2

2 1 2 3 4 3 2

5 2 4 6

Twinkle Twinkle Little Star

6 6 2 2 1 1 2

3 3 4 4 5 5 6

2 2 3 3 4 4 5

2 2 3 3 4 4 5

6 6 2 2 1 1 2

3 3 4 4 5 5 6

Alouette

3 2 1 1 2 3 2 1 3 6

3 2 1 1 2 3 2 1 3

Jingle Bells

4 4 4 4 4 4 4 2 6 5 4

3 3 3 3 3 4 4 4 4 5 5 4 5 2

4 4 4 4 4 4 4 2 6 5 4

3 3 3 3 3 4 4 4 4 2 2 3 5 6

So far, all the tunes played have been in the key of D, the penny whistle's 'own' key. Using a D penny whistle it is also possible to play tunes in the key of G. This key introduces another note, C (in the third illustration on page 9, C sharp (C#) is shown). C is written thus in musical notation:

C on stave

To play C, remove all your fingers from the holes except the left middle and ring fingers:

Penny whistle playing C

The following tune is in the key of G, and uses C.

The bottom illustration on page 9 referred to overblowing, the technique used to reach the notes one octave (eight notes) above those featured already. To produce these higher notes, blow normally with all the holes covered, then slightly increase the pressure of air until the same note sounds, but higher. Stop and try to produce the high note from the start; tonguing the note helps here. Once you make this octave note regularly, move up the notes as shown on page 19.

The advantage of being able to play the high octave is demonstrated by playing 'Frère Jacques' high, bringing in one note from the lower octave.

Practise playing the tunes on the previous pages in the high octave. They may sound shrill at the beginning, but work at getting an even sound; try alternating between the low and high octaves as well.

Good Night, Ladies

1 3 6 3 1 3 1 2

1 3 0/2 0/2 0/2 1 3 2 4 3

1 2 3 2 1 1 1

2 2 2 1 ⑥ ⑥

1 2 3 2 1 1 1

2 2 1 2 3

Frère Jacques in high octave

⑥ ⑤ ④ ⑥ ⑥ ⑤ ④ ⑥

④ ③ ② ④ ③ ②

② ① ② ③ ④ ⑥

② ① ② ③ ④ ⑥

⑥ 2 ⑥ ⑥ 2 ⑥

Beats and time

So far, the tunes that you have played are so well-known that their rhythms will have come to you as second nature. But what happens when you are faced with unfamiliar tunes? This is where a basic knowledge of reading music comes in handy.

Even a tune as simple as 'Frère Jacques' uses three different lengths of note and a system of counting the notes. If you imagine that each phrase of the song is one bar or measure, this can be counted in fours:

Frère Jacques

1 2 3 4 1 2 3 4
Frè - re Jac - ques, Frè - re Jac - ques,

1 2 3 4 1 2 3 4
Dor - mez - vous? Dor - mez - vous?

1 2 3 4 1 2 3 4
Son- nez les ma- tin - es, Son- nez les ma- tin - es,

1 2 3 4 1 2 3 4
Ding Dang Dong, Ding Dang Dong.

The three types of notes used are a quarter note, or crochet, equal to one beat, a half note, or minim, equal to two beats, and an eighth note, or quaver, equal to a half beat. In musical notation, they are written:

♩ quarter note or crochet – **1 beat**

𝅗𝅥 half note or minim – **2 beats**

♪ eighth note or quaver – **½ beat**

Using these notes, 'Frère Jacques' looks like this:

Frè - re Jac - ques, Frè - re Jac - ques,

Dor - mez - vous? Dor - mez - vous?

Son- nez les ma- tin - es, Son- nez les ma- tin - es,

Ding Dang Dong, Ding Dang Dong.

There are, of course, many other beats used, and these will be included in some of the examples later in this chapter. For now, a brief description of the main two will suffice:

whole note or semibreve – **4 beats**

sixteenth note or semiquaver – **¼ beat**

As well as knowing the notation of the beats, you also need to know how a rest, when no notes are played, is shown:

semibreve rest – **4 beats**

minim rest – **2 beats**

crochet rest – **1 beat**

quaver rest – **½ beat**

semiquaver rest – **¼ beat**

Many tunes, particularly traditional jigs and reels, use dotted notes, where the beat is extended:

dotted half note or dotted minim – **3 beats**

dotted quaver note or crochet – **1½ beats**

dotted eighth note or quaver – **¾ beat**

The exercises below are designed to help you familiarize yourself with reading notes and rests. It is a good idea to keep the beat with your foot while you are playing.

Exercise 1

Exercise 2

Exercise 3

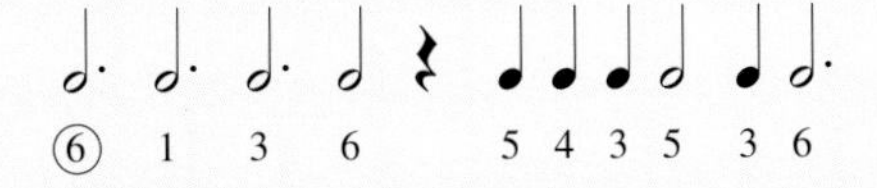

Exercise 4

4 6 5 6 4 5 6 6 6 4 3 2 2 1 2 5

Reading music

Now that you know what the notes are in terms of beats, it is a relatively easy matter to show how they link up with the notes you play on the penny whistle. The music theory given here is designed to help you play tunes in the key of D major and G major, both of which are easy on a D penny whistle; there are many good books available to help you understand other keys and further your knowledge of theory.

Musical notation is written on staves, which consist of five parallel horizontal lines enclosing four spaces, all of which are used for notes:

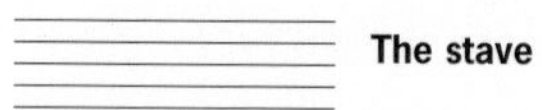

The stave

Most music is written using one or two staves; the penny whistle uses the treble, or higher, clef, and music for piano or guitar also uses the bass, or lower clef:

The Treble Clef

The Bass Clef

The note on the treble clef correspond to those played on a penny whistle, while those in the bass clef are most commonly played by piano or guitar.

Notes on treble and bass staves, including C and C#

The example of notes on the treble clef on the previous page can be played, but a long stream of notes gives no idea of where to put the emphasis that gives life to a tune. To help you find the structure of a tune, the stave is divided up into bars or measures by vertical lines called bar lines. The first note after the bar line is emphasized. A double bar line denotes the end of a tune, while a 'dotted' double bar line at the beginning and end of a tune means that it is repeated.

Bar, double bar, and 'dotted' double bar lines

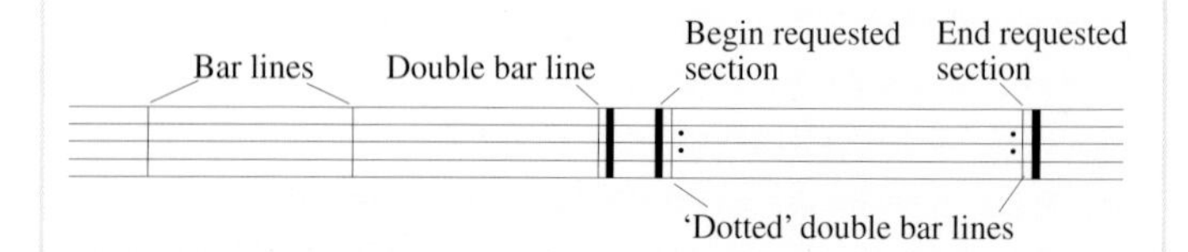

What goes in each bar is determined by the time signature. This is made up of two numbers, one of top of the other. The number on the top is for the number of beats in each measure, and the number on the bottom is for the type of note getting each beat. The latter relates to the notes shown on page 27, and the most often used number is 4, which stands for four crochets. It is theoretically possible to write music in almost any combination of time signatures – but not to play it! The signatures shown below are used in nearly all tunes in the fields of folk, country and rock music.

Standard time signatures

$\frac{2}{4}$ Two crochets per bar; this is used for fast times, and it is faster than $\frac{4}{4}$

$\frac{3}{4}$ Three crochets per bar; otherwise known as 'waltz time', as all waltzes are in this signature

$\frac{4}{4}$ Four crochets per bar; the most used time signature in non-classical western musics, particularly for marching time and blues

$\frac{6}{8}$ Six quavers per bar; played with the emphasis on the first and fourth notes, this gives a jaunty, hornpipe feel

The key signature at the beginning of a tune tells you what notes should be played each time, unless instructed otherwise. These are related to the notes on a keyboard; white keys are called the 'Naturals', and black keys 'accidentals' (sharps and flats). The key of D has two sharps in its scale – the notes are D, E, F#, G, A, B and C# – so a piece of music that has two sharps corresponding to these notes before the time signature will be in this key. A D penny whistle also plays tunes in the key of G major; here, the notes of the scale are G, A, B, C, D, E and F#, so a tune in this key has one sharp on the note F.

In theory, any penny whistle can be used to play in all keys, but in reality this demands a ridiculously complicated technique. If you want to play in other keys, you should buy penny whistles in those keys (*see* page 8). The key signatures for D and G are given below; all the tunes in this book are in one of these keys.

Within a tune, a note may have a sharp – ♯ – or flat – ♭ – sign next to it; this denotes that that note should be played sharp or flat within that bar, whatever the key signature. A 'natural' sign – ♮ – next to a note means that it should not be played as a sharp or flat, whatever the key signature; if there is no natural sign next to the note the next time it appears in the tune, it should be played as a sharp or flat as usual.

Key signatures

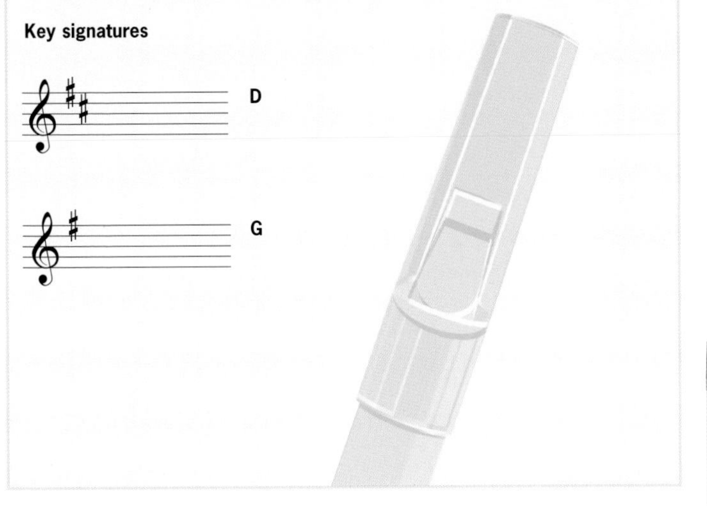

Scales and arpeggios

Practising scales is the best way of learning how to find any single note on any instrument; for fluency, it is no less than vital.

Start with a scale of D on the bottom octave:

Then practise the top octave on its own, before adding it to the bottom one, and then practise the scale of G:

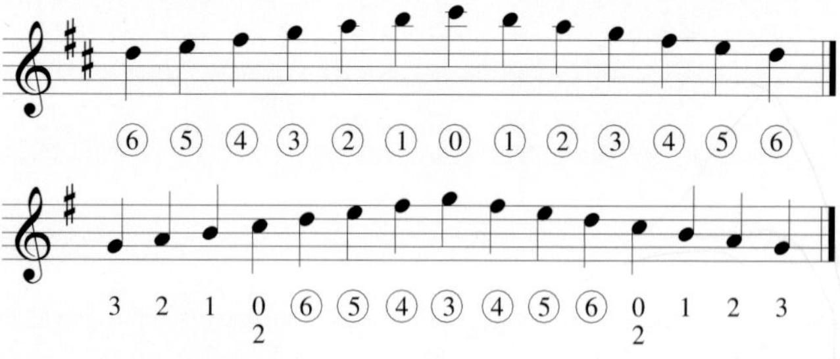

Arpeggios are the four single notes that make up chords in a key; in the key of D, they are D, F#, A and D. Play the arpeggios of the bottom octave as shown below, then add the top octave as before. In the key of G, the notes of the arpeggio are G, B, D and G.

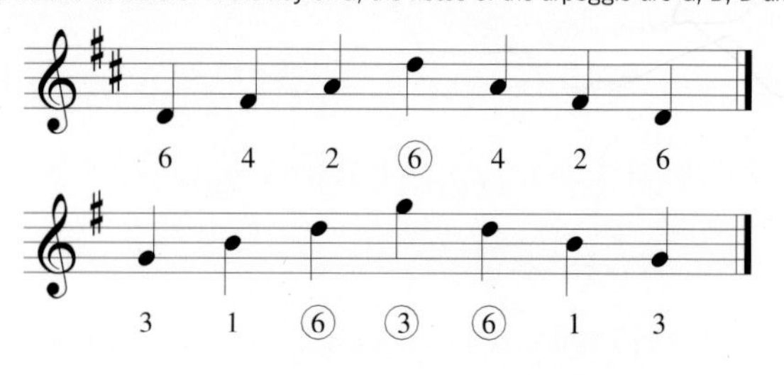

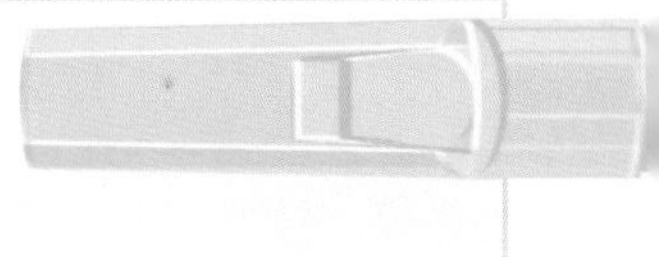

Putting it all together

The musical theory in the previous pages may have seemed like hard work, getting in the way of what you really want to do – play the penny whistle. However, once you start expanding your repertoire you will find it vital when you come to gathering new tunes to play; penny whistle notation is only used in instruction books such as this, and you're on your own after that. In addition, being able to read and play a piece of music can lead to all sorts of unexpected delights and discoveries – you may find yourself faced with a tune without a title or that you've never heard of, and being able to interpret it is a very useful skill.

To test your knowledge, try playing this short tune, written without any penny whistle notation:

Recognize it? It won't come round again, as you move onto tunes that incorporate all the theory and techniques you've learnt so far. As you go through the tunes, work on your interpretation of each one – it is all very well being able to play the right notes in the correct rhythm, but that is less than half of what makes an interesting musical performance. Try playing the tunes at different tempos, or speeds – fast, slow and in-between – and see whether tonguing the notes or letting them flow sounds more appropriate for the tune; this process of exploration once you are familiar with the written notes adds enjoyment and proficiency to your playing.

Au Clair de la Lune

3 3 3 2 1 2 3 1 2 2 3

3 3 3 2 1 2 3 1 2 2 3

2 2 2 2 5 5 2 3 4 5 6

3 3 3 2 1 2 3 1 2 2 3

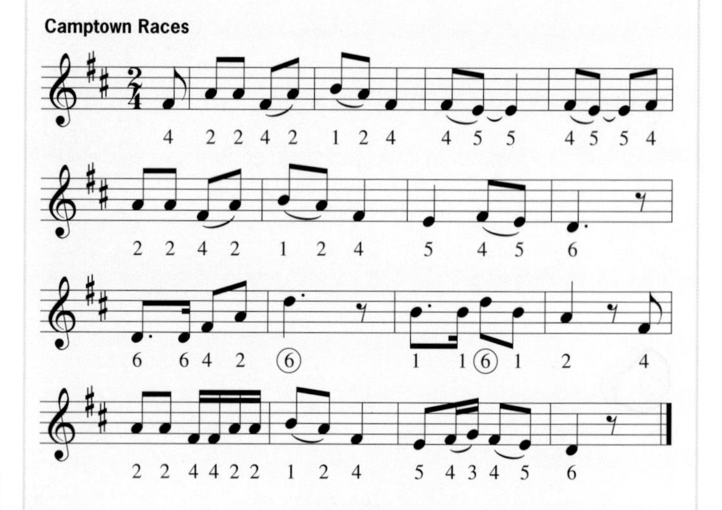

Oh My Darling Clementine
3 3 3 6 1 1 1 3 3 1 ⑥ ⑥ 0 1
2 2 1 0 0 1 2 1 3 3 1 2 6 4 2 3
2 2
Molly Malone
6 3 3 3 3 1 3 3 2 2 2 2 0 1 2
2
1 2 3 ⑥ 0 1 1 2 3 2 6
2
3 3 3 3 1 3 2 2 2 2 0 1 2
2
1 ⑥ 0 1 ⑥ 0 1 3 2 3
2 2

Scarborough Fair

The Old Folks at Home

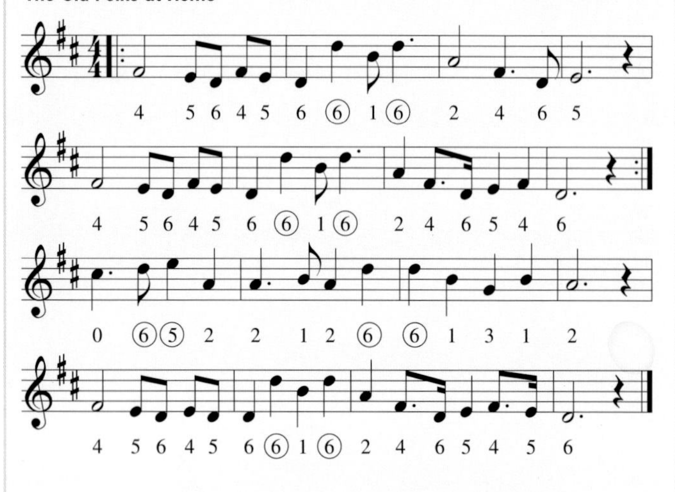

Annie Laurie
6 6 6 ⑥ ⑥ 0 1 1 2 4 4 5 6 5 5 4 5
6 6 ⑥ ⑥ 0 1 1 2 4 4 5 6 2
⑥ ⑥⑤ ⑤ ④ 2 ⑥ ⑥⑤ ⑤④ ④ ⑤
⑥ 0 1 ⑥1 2 4 4 5 6 ⑥ 4 4 5 6
Early One Morning
3 3 3 3 1 ⑥ ⑥ ⑤ 0/2 2 3 4 2 6 6
3 3 3 3 1 ⑥ ⑥ ⑤ 0/2 2 4 3
2 1 0/2 ⑥ 1 3 2 1 0/2 ⑥ 1 3
3 1 ⑥ ③ ④ ⑤ ⑥ 0/2 1 2 3 4 3

Auld Lang Syne
6 3 3 3 1 2 3 2 1 3 3 1 6
5 5 6 1 1 3 2 3 2 1 3 5 5 6
3 5 6 1 1 3 2 3 2 1 6 1 1 6
5 5 6 1 1 3 2 3 2 1 3 5 5 6 3
Oh! Suzanna
3 2 1 6 6 5 6 1 3 2 1 1 2 3
2 3 2 1 6 6 5 6 1 3 2 1 1 2 2
3 3 2 1 6 6 5 6 1 3 2 1 1 2 3
2 3 2 1 6 6 5 6 1 3 2 1 1 2 2

3 0 2 0 2 5 5 5 6 6 1 3 2 3 2
1 6 6 5 6 1 3 2 1 1 2 2 3
Coming Thro' the Rye
6 6 6 1 2 3 2 1 6 6 5 6
3 6 6 6 1 2 3 2 1
6 6 5 6 3 6 1 3 1 2 3 2 1
6 1 3 1 6 5 5 6 1 0 2 2

Amazing Grace

Swing Low, Sweet Chariot

3 3 3 3 1 1 (6) (6) (6) (5) (6) 1 1 3
3 3 3 3 5 6 3 3 3 3 1 1 2 3

Daisy Bell

(6) 1 3 6 5 4 3 5 3
6 2 (6) 1 3 5 4 3
2 1 2 1 0 1 2 (6) 1 2 3
2
2 1 3 5 3 5 6 6 3 1 2
3 1 2 1 0 (6) 1 3 2 6 3
2

The British Grenadiers
6 3 6 3 2 1 2 1 0 2 ⑥ 3 1 2 3 4
3 6 3 6 3 2 1 2 1 0 2 ⑥ 3 1 2 3 4
3 1 0 2 ⑥ ⑤ ⑥ 0 2 1 0 2 ⑥ ⑥
⑤ ⑤ ⑥ 0 2 1 2 3 4 6 3 6 3 2
1 2 1 0 2 ⑥ 3 1 2 3 4 3

Loch Lomond

My Love is like a Red, Red Rose

Londonderry Air

Chapter **3**

Advanced techniques and tunes

'Tom with his pipe made
such a noise
That he pleased both the girls
and boys
And they all stopped to hear him play,
"Over the Hills and Far Away".

'Tom with his pipe did play with
such skill
That those who heard him could never
keep still;
As soon as he played they began for
to dance
Even pigs on their hind legs would after
him prance.'

Seventeenth-century nursery rhyme

A mainstay of the Chieftains for many years, Paddy Moloney's whistle-playing can be heard on many recordings.

Ornamentation and taking tunes further

This chapter is about progressing from being a player of tunes on the penny whistle to being a penny whistle player. If you have worked at and mastered the basic tunes on pages 34 to 45, you may be wondering how to make them sound like your own interpretation and take them further – even if making pigs dance is not your ultimate musical ambition. The following hints and tips are part of the penny whistle player's repertoire; listen to as many people as you can, and you will undoubtedly pick up more.

Trilling, as its name indicates, is a technique for imitating the trill of birdsong. With four fingerholes covered, blow the note and flick your right index finger up and down on the hole quickly; you don't need to raise the finger far off the hole. Practise this with each finger in turn – the ring fingers may need more work than the others – making sure you achieve enough control to regulate the trill as you wish: long or short, or many or few notes. As with the other ornamentation techniques described here, trills are effective when used sparingly, but they can become cloying and repetitious very soon if they are played constantly throughout a piece.

Sometimes known as the cut, grace notes, used infrequently, add interest to a tune. Like trills, they are of ancient origin and are found in many types of Western music; they are an introductory note played in hardly any time before another one, and are written thus:

Grace note

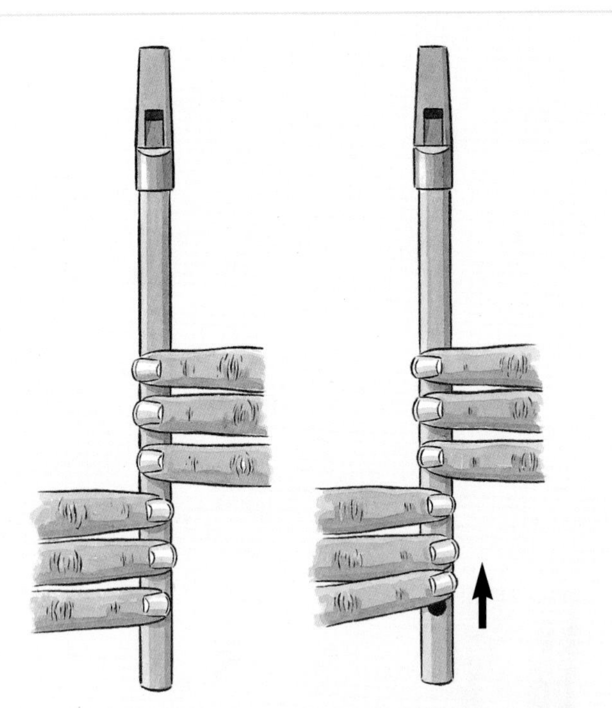

Sliding from one note to another, sometimes via a semitone, is a particularly effective technique for slow tunes, although there is no reason why you can't use it in quicker pieces. Start by covering all six fingerholes, then blow and, instead of raising the finger on hole 6, slide it upwards and off, producing a smooth transition between the notes.

When you can do this fluently, practise sliding up between all the holes, and then work on sliding downwards, to lower the note.

The tunes in the following section are written in their basic form – it is up to you to find and play any appropriate ornamentation. A selection of influential players is given on page 58, and it is worth listening to recordings to see how each one embellishes a tune, if at all. You will also notice that the penny whistle notation has disappeared – don't worry, but take time to practise your sight-reading.

Sweeny's Polka
The Merry Blacksmith

Shandon Bells
1.
2.

Sean McKenna's No 1
Sean McKenna's No 2

3
Ballydesmond
1.
2.
1.
2.

Peg Ryan's Polka
Shaalds o'Foula

Villafjord

Monaghan's Jig
Give Me Your Hand

When the Tide comes in
The Lark in the Morning

Players and influences

It would be impossible to make a comprehensive list of great penny whistle players – it would take up too much of the book, and the problem with trying to be all-inclusive is that someone's favourite is bound to slip through the net. So the names included here have been chosen because they have all used the penny whistle adventurously and in perfect harmony with their chosen styles of music.

It has also proved very difficult to compile a discography, because in some cases the albums are out of print, or different companies have released the same record in different countries, or because re-releases may be of inferior quality. However, all these players are worth seeking out for their approach to playing; even if the type of music doesn't appeal to you, listen to how they use the penny whistle and enjoy all the sounds and emotions that can be coaxed from this little instrument!

Most recorded penny whistle players have been Irish or have played in Irish traditional styles: Paddy Moloney of the Chieftains, Willie Clancy of the Clancy Brothers and fiddler/whistle player Frankie Gavin of De Dannan are among the best-known, because of their many tours and records. Mary Bergin, James McNally, John McSherry, Seamus Egan and Sean Ryan are among the foremost current Irish players, and the playing of Packie Byrne and Miko Russell recalls the older traditional styles. Paul Brady, more regarded as a singer/guitarist, has also recorded penny whistle tunes.

The penny whistle in Scottish music is well represented on record by bands such as the Whistlebinkies, Ceolbeg and Deaf Shepherd, and Robin Williamson's penny whistle playing has been a feature of his career, from the Incredible String Band through to his many solo albums. There are also many recordings in which the penny whistle appears, but not as a lead melodic instrument.

Frankie Gavin of De Dannan playing in traditional mode.

Index of tunes